THREE TREES

A Play by Alvin Eng

*A Dramatic Portrait of Isaku Yanaihara,
Annette and Alberto Giacometti*

No Passport Press

*For Wendy, the muse of this play and my life
…remembering the magic of "meeting" Isaku and Alberto on our
Parisian honeymoon.*

For performance rights enquiries, please contact the author at
www.alvineng.com

Cover Design by Zonia Tsang

Detail of "The Three Trees"
etching by Rembrandt van Rijn

No Passport Press (founding editor: Caridad Svich)
PO Box 1786, South Gate, CA 90280 USA.
Website: https://www.nopassport.org
Email: NoPassportPress@aol.com

ISBN: 978-1-716-30790-4

ABOUT PORTRAIT PLAYS

THREE TREES is the first of Alvin Eng's *Portrait Plays* cycle of historical dramas that examine the parallels between portraiture, history and power as manifested in the convergence of different disciplines, eras and cultures. The play explores the haunting relationship between Alberto Giacometti, one of the most influential artists of the 20th century, and his primary 1950s muse/model, Japanese philosopher & professor Isaku Yanaihara.

The second work, 33 & 1/3 **CORNELIA STREET** dramatizes the fateful events that forever bonded the legacies of bohemian Greenwich Village legends, Joe Gould, proto-Beat poet and controversial oral history figure, and Joseph Mitchell, renowned writer for *The New Yorker Magazine*, through the powerful vortex of revered painter Alice Neel's groundbreaking portrait of Gould. Alternating between 1930s Greenwich Village and a 1970s Women's Studies lecture by accidental feminist icon, Neel, the play explores the conflicts of spiritual vs. commercial ownership of a work of art, as well as that of personal stories that become published, public history.

THE IMPERIAL IMAGE, the third Portrait Play, is a dramatic triptych probing the powerful role of portraits in societal structures and rituals—from the court of Emperor Akbar the Great in Mughal era India to Marie Antoinette and Catherine the Great's court portraitist, Elisabeth Vigée LeBrun, to Shepard Fairey's creation of the ubiquitous "Hope" poster for Barack Obama's 2008 campaign.

Dramaturg for the *Portrait Plays* cycle: Wendy Wasdahl

In 2012, THREE TREES had two English language presentations in Paris. Moving Parts Theatre presented a staged reading of the play. Selected scenes were also presented at the Sorbonne's conference, *&Now 2012 New Writing in Paris: Exchanges and Cross-Fertilizations*.

THREE TREES had its World Premiere Off-Broadway with the Pan Asian Repertory Theatre, Tisa Chang, Artistic Producing Director.
The production ran from March 23 - April 14, 2013 at the West End Theatre, NYC, directed by Ernest Abuba

CAST (in order of appearance)

ISAKU YANAIHARA	*Marcus Ho*
ALBERTO GIACOMETTI	*Jean-Pierre Stewart*
ANNETTE GIACOMETTI	*Leah Cogan*
DIEGO GIACOMETTI	*Scott Klavan*

In 2016, Baltimore Center Stage presented the play in a workshop production directed by Hana S. Sharif.

"*Three Trees* is an astonishingly moving play about Alberto Giacometti, his wife Annette, his brother, Diego, and his good friend, Isaku Yanaihara. Eng has perfectly captured the personalities of each as well as the steamy and stormy interactions that wove them into a tight triangle. Eng's deep appreciation for and comprehension of Giacometti's art sheds a brilliant light on the complex human drama that unfolds before our eyes."
LAURIE WILSON,
Author of *Alberto Giacometti: Myth Magic and the Man*

"*Three Trees* is a magic wand that wishes the past into the present. I was often with Alberto and company from 1949 to 1961. I had intimate talks with all the actors there. This play moves me in the deepest way by how well it recalls those challenging and so rewarding times."
HERBERT LUST
Author of *Giacometti: The Complete Graphics and a frequent model himself for Giacometti*

FOREWORD

by Hana S. Sharif

I was first introduced to Alvin Eng's writing through the beautiful, existential beginning of the *Portrait Plays Cycle*, *Three Trees*. As the metaphoric layers of history began to unfurl in the opening moments of the play, I found myself swept away by the elegance and depth of our journey into these four intersecting lives.

As we entered rehearsal for a workshop of *Three Trees*, I was struck by the realization that in the quiet grace of Alvin's voice, there was a ferocity of intellectual rigor and fearlessness to deconstruct the complexity of the artistic journey. Melding darkness and light, hubris and vulnerability, genius and madness, muses and mastery, Alvin Eng's world swirled to life.

Few artists could so clearly elucidate the feeling of being consumed, compelled, and captivated by the creation process, delving deeply into the physical, psychic, and spiritual cost of the act of manifesting. If the goal of an artist is to create the ephemeral and eternal, then undoubtedly these pages stand as a testament to the deft and powerful mind of Alvin Eng.

Hana S. Sharif is the Artistic Director of The Repertory Theatre of St. Louis

INTRODUCTION

by Alvin Eng

Shortly after the turn of the 21st century, I became fascinated with the act and power dynamics of portraiture. After all, no matter the medium or whether the work is linear or non-linear, representational or abstract, harmonic, atonal or dissonant, or any combination thereof, all artists aspire to create portraits that explore and illuminate aspects of the human condition that stir the soul.

Looking at the process of painted and sculpted portraits in particular, who wields more influence over what emerges on the paper, canvas or clay—the model or the sitter? Then, there's the question of spiritual as opposed to commercial ownership. Who, ultimately, inhabits that portrait's soul? As a playwright, I started exploring how to dramatize this creative act, as well as these existential questions, for the stage. As the visible, exterior portion of this act is largely a static, sedentary process, this was proving to be a quite a challenging task.

In January 2008, on my honeymoon in Paris, on a morning when all the Parisian papers blared the headline, "Obama: New JFK?," my newlywed wife, Wendy, and I attended the exhibition, *Alberto Giacometti: Atelier,* at Centre Pompidou. Upon entering the gallery, we were immediately transfixed and transformed by the sight of the actual walls that were salvaged from Giacometti's legendary atelier at 46 Rue de Hippolyte-Maindron—just a few blocks away.

The first wall copy I happened to read was about his relationship with his primary muse and model of the late 1950s, Japanese philosopher and professor, Isaku Yanaihara. This relationship forever haunted and changed both men's lives, as well as Giacometti's work and his relationship with his wife, Annette, and brother/aide-de-camp, Diego. I immediately knew that I had finally found the vessel with which to dramatize the act of portraiture.

Now, almost midway through the second year of the third decade of the new millennium, there have been many theatrical performances of THREE TREES. I even had the pleasure of reading the role of Isaku at a 2012 writing conference at The Sorbonne in the very same city in which the play first took shape and where it, ultimately, takes place. Now, I thank you for taking this journey on the page. As I write this, we are also a year into the pandemic. I hope there will be more opportunities to experience this play on the stage as well.

Thank you to each and every one of the artists, administrators, educators and audiences who so generously shared their talent and time to make this play come alive over all these years.

Finally, this play would not exist without the love, inspiration and steadfast dramaturgical research and input from my wife of now over a decade, Wendy Wasdahl.

CHARACTERS
(in order of appearance)

ISAKU YANAIHARA – Male, ages 38-47. Japanese existential philosopher and scholar from a renowned, controversial Tokyo family. Isaku is the first non-family member to become a recurring muse/model in Giacometti's insular world.

ALBERTO GIACOMETTI –Male, ages 54-65 of Swiss descent. World-renowned 20th Century master sculptor. Obsessively focused on his work to the detriment of his physical and emotional well-being.

ANNETTE GIACOMETTI – Female, ages 33-42, of Swiss descent. Alberto's wife and muse/model. After a decade of being married to Alberto, she is ready to redefine the parameters of their unique union.

DIEGO GIACOMETTI –Male, ages 53-64. Alberto's younger brother, of Swiss descent, protector, muse/model and studio aide-de-camp. An artist in his own right, Diego creates all of the foundations and finishing layers for his brother's sculptures.

SETTINGS: Isaku's meditation room, Tokyo, 1966; Alberto's studio, Café Didot and Annette's apartment, Paris, 1956-1960.

PROLOGUE

Tokyo, January 11, 1966. ISAKU sits in his Meditation Room before a bust that bears his likeness. He is draped in a mourning kimono.

ISAKU: A great artist died last night. Part of me died with him. My existence will one day come to an end. But thanks to the great artist, my essence will live on. It is the Maestro's genius that realized this head from the dust of clay, but it is my soul that radiates through it. This bust is as much a result of what I brought out of him, as what he brought out of me. Tonight, I will honor him in his death as I did in his life by sitting perfectly still for as long as I can . . . Some call this modeling. For me this is sitting meditation. Though we have not been in the same room for over five years, not a single day goes by where I do not sit like this and imagine that I am still in Paris, sitting for the Maestro. That was as close to pure love as I will ever know.

End of Prologue: Transition to Scene 1

ACT I - Scene 1

ISAKU's Meditation Room transforms into ALBERTO's 12 x 15-foot studio, Paris, 1956. The studio looks like a war zone. The carnage of creation wars is strewn all over the floor. The walls are full of assorted, random black, gray and white sketches. ISAKU sits in the same spot as during the Prologue. When the transition is complete, ISAKU rises, removes his mourning kimono to reveal a 1950s style tweed western business suit.

ISAKU: Maestro, are you here? . . . Maestro?

> *(ALBERTO enters. His ragged tweed and gray flannel suit is covered in dust and looking very ghost-like. He walks with a slight imbalance and is carrying several wet towels. He wraps the towels around sculptures-in-progress, making them look like mummies. He locks eyes with ISAKU and engages him in a long handshake.)*

ALBERTO: Professor, welcome back! It's been an unusually cold September. The plaster is drying up so quickly that I have to use wet towels to keep the sculptures . . . alive I was going to say.

ISAKU: Alive they are.

ALBERTO: . . . I'll be right back.

> *(ALBERTO exits. ISAKU becomes entranced with the works-in-progress. ALBERTO re-enters. He has dusted off his suit, but it still looks very worked in—maybe even slept in. His tie is properly knotted up to the collar.)*

ALBERTO: Thank you for coming back to sit for me.

ISAKU: Maestro, to be in your presence once again is my greatest honor. To be allowed entry to your sacred studio . . . words will never describe my gratitude.

ALBERTO: My wife, Annette, thinks it's a dirty hovel. Now. She loved it when she first got here.

ISAKU: It is a woman's prerogative to change her mind.

ALBERTO: The brothels are the only place where man and woman can truly be free. Everything is in the open and the Madame gives you the bill up front.

ISAKU: We all pay the price in the end.

ALBERTO: Absolutely . . . Cigarette?

ISAKU: Maybe afterwards, thank you.

ALBERTO: Let's begin with a drawing. Please, sit right over there.

> *(ISAKU sits. ALBERTO lights up the first of a succession of cigarettes and settles into his drawing spot. They sit knee to knee. He places a large drawing pad on his lap. They lock eyes intensely for a long period of time. ALBERTO starts drawing.)*

ALBERTO: Eyes to me . . . A little higher . . . Please hold that . . . Beautiful . . . Formidable . . . Your face is like a new country to me—and I don't mean Japan.

ISAKU: You will find my face boring in no time at all.

ALBERTO: It's not what is seen, it's how one sees it.

ISAKU: I have always been fascinated by the process of creation.

ALBERTO: Fascination quickly becomes frustration. Whatever I cannot control, I destroy. I have destroyed far more than I will ever create.

ISAKU: So, you will either control me or destroy me.

ALBERTO: Or you will control or destroy me.

ISAKU: Is there no alternative to control or destroy?

ALBERTO: If there is, I haven't found it. My greatest frustration is that most models cannot sustain the level of concentration needed to achieve this alchemy. Besides Annette and my brother, Diego, most models get self-conscious and wind-up quitting on me.

ISAKU: Hegel believes that consciousness of an other or an object, is, in itself, self-consciousness.

ALBERTO: The state of being self-conscious is far inferior to achieving a state of self-consciousness. I helped illustrate Kojeve's study of Hegel.

ISAKU: Your illustrations were exemplary. My dissertation was on Hegel.

ALBERTO: I hope you turn out to be as good a model as you are a philosopher.

ISAKU: I will try my best.

>   *(ALBERTO continues drawing. Time passes . . . he abruptly stops.)*

ALBERTO: . . . I've lost you.

ISAKU: Did I speak out of turn?

ALBERTO: I've forgotten how to draw. I don't even know how to look! I may as well be back in The Academy in 1925—I have learned nothing since. This is useless. All these years of looking and I still see nothing!

ISAKU: Do you need a rest?

ALBERTO: Usually the models are begging me to stop. You're the first to ask if I need a rest. I have to wet these towels again. Excuse me.

(ALBERTO exits. ISAKU becomes even more entranced with the works-in-progress. ALBERTO returns with more wet towels that he re-wraps over the sculptures.)

ISAKU: Your new sculptures . . . are more alive with motion . . . yet pulsing with death . . . It's as if they embody that thin line between death and life.

ALBERTO: Since meeting you last winter . . . Every time I close my eyes . . . sometimes even with my eyes wide open . . . I still see the death camp survivors . . . their hollow eyes, blank expression . . . I used to walk by them at the Hotel Lutetia . . . After the war, motion pictures stopped being a series of images . . . to me, they became a barrage of dots . . .yet when the death camp survivors appeared on the newsreels . . . I could see their emaciated bodies . . . clear as day . . . they were like walking spirits. . . spirits embodying the essence of violence.

ISAKU: To exist in violence is to exist closer to death than to life. Too many of my family, my friends and classmates are disfigured or dead. When I look at your work, I feel their spirits moving through me again.

ALBERTO: We cannot bring them all back to life, but we can try.

ISAKU: The Egyptians regard a sculptor as "one who keeps alive."

ALBERTO: Magic. That is one of my core beliefs.

ISAKU: You have a strong core.

ALBERTO: We will see if my core is as strong as yours. Here we are. Please Sit. Show me your eyes . . . A little higher . . . Please hold that.

(ALBERTO resumes drawing.)

ISAKU: I am glad it was only a temporary setback.

ALBERTO: Starting again is never a problem. Finishing is much more difficult.

ISAKU: Some artists equate completion with death.

ALBERTO: I equate inactivity with death. I am very afraid of dying. I was only nineteen when I saw a man die before my very eyes. I was traveling with an elderly Dutchman. At our first dinner, he started complaining of chest pains. Luckily, the hotel had a doctor on staff. After examining him, the doctor told me his heart was failing and there was nothing to be done. Nothing to be done! I started reading to him. When he started to lose consciousness, I started to draw him . . . It was all I could do to try to keep him alive . . . save something permanent from this man, this living being who was about to become a lifeless object . . . If I can see a face on a canvas or in a sculpture it is alive. When I can no longer see it, it no longer exists.

ISAKU: Thank you for bringing me to life.

ALBERTO: Thank you for keeping me alive. Are you married?

ISAKU: Why do you ask?

ALBERTO: I've not once had to ask you to be still.

ISAKU: Is that a trait of marriage?

ALBERTO: Only of a good marriage.

ISAKU: Thank you, I am married. We have two daughters.

ALBERTO: Have you ever sat for a portrait before?

ISAKU: Never.

ALBERTO: There is nothing more powerful than a first sitting. My father, Giovanni, was a painter. When we were children, he would pose me with my brother, Diego, and our sister, Otillia. All three of us were naked. I remember father's gaze penetrating right through me.

ISAKU: My first sitting is much simpler than yours.

ALBERTO: For a first-time sitter, you are extraordinary

ISAKU: I know my purpose—at home and, hopefully, in this studio.

ALBERTO: I wish I knew my purpose . . . anywhere—
Damn! This isn't working.

ISAKU: Is everything all right?

ALBERTO: I should check this morning's sculptures
again.

(*ISAKU stands and stretches. ALBERTO unwraps some
of the sculptures-in-progress.*)

ALBERTO: They're starting to come alive.

ISAKU: May I see?

ALBERTO: Later—please don't be insulted.

ISAKU: Not at all.

(*ALBERTO resumes drawing.*)

ALBERTO: Let's get back . . . Show me your eyes . . . A
little bit lower . . . Right to me . . . Please hold that.
There . . . Yes . . . Perfect . . . It's like I'm drawing for the
first time . . . Remembering how to look . . . maybe I will
remember how to see . . . maybe one day the world will
remember how to see . . . the barriers between art and
life, art and death, society and convention, will be
eradicated . . . In every museum and city square, they
will remove the sculptures from their pedestals and
replace them with prostitutes! Prostitutes are living,
breathing sculptures. They do more for a city's psyche
than dead art objects ever will.

ISAKU: Does your wife share this belief?

ALBERTO: Of course, she does. Annette has accompanied me to The Sphinx many times. If only all Parisians and all artists learned the lessons of The Sphinx. If I had met you ten years earlier, I would have surely taken you to The Sphinx.

ISAKU: Did you make regular sojourns to Egypt?

ALBERTO: Professor, The Sphinx was a brothel in the next arrondissement. It was truly a liberating place, a social equalizer bar none. Losing the Sphinx was one of the major casualties that Paris suffered in the war. Professor, have you availed yourself of the wonderful brothels of Boulevard Montparnasse?

ISAKU: Maestro, I am married.

ALBERTO: Professor, so am I. Annette knows everything about me.

ISAKU: Well I am sorry to have missed The Sphinx of Paris. But I plan to visit the original Sphinx in Egypt on my way home to Japan next week.

ALBERTO: Aaaarrrraaagghh! NO! You cannot leave me!

ISAKU: I have completed my research. My flight is on September fifteenth.

ALBERTO: Until I can draw your face, nothing will be the same. Professor, I need you to stay longer. You cannot leave Paris.

ISAKU: I will see what I can do.

ALBERTO: I should check this morning's sculptures again.

> (ALBERTO unwraps the towels from that day's sculptures and examines them . . . then destroys the drawings and sculptures.)

ISAKU: What's wrong?

ALBERTO: Everything I did today was useless . . . completely false.

ISAKU: Why don't we keep working?

ALBERTO: Let's go to Café Didot. Those works were only meant to exist for a brief time.

ISAKU: Maestro . . . hold on to the pieces.

> End of scene.

Act I – Scene 2

Café Didot a few minutes later. ALBERTO and ISAKU are dining, reading newspapers.

ALBERTO: Café Didot is our kitchen, our dining room and our parlour. Annette, Diego and I take most of our meals here. We even receive telegrams and telephone calls here.

ISAKU: How convenient.

ALBERTO: Right across the street—it's actually closer than the communal latrine we share with the other artists.

(ANNETTE enters.)

ANNETTE: Alberto? You're here so early.

ALBERTO: As usual, I was accomplishing nothing at the studio. Annette, you remember Professor Yanaihara. Last year he interviewed me for the Japanese magazine.

ANNETTE: Of course. Lovely to see you again, Professor.

ISAKU: The pleasure is mine.

ANNETTE: Professor, we would love to read your article. Would you mind translating it for us?

ISAKU: It would be my honor.

ALBERTO: The Professor is a brilliant translator. He translated Camus' "The Stranger" and many works of Kierkegaard into Japanese.

ISAKU: I am flattered that you remembered.

ALBERTO: They are significant accomplishments.

ANNETTE: Have you written other books?

ISAKU: Only more translations.

ALBERTO: All art is translation. The whole world is translation. Look at today's newspaper. If only France, Great Britain and Egypt could translate each other's needs over the Suez, let alone understand each other . . . Ugh, Eden, Mollet and Nasser will take us straight back to war.

ANNETTE: Alberto is always preparing for the worst. Are you enjoying your stay in Paris?

ISAKU: Everything worthwhile in art and life is here in Paris.

ALBERTO: Then why are you leaving me?

ISAKU: My research grant has already been extended a year. It's time.

ANNETTE: What is the focus of your research?

ISAKU: French Existential Philosophy.

ALBERTO: He is too modest. Professor is in residence at the Sorbonne. He knows Camus, he knows Sartre.

ISAKU: I have yet to meet Monsieur Sartre. He and Camus had a major falling-out just as I arrived. But I would love to meet him.

ALBERTO: Jean Paul is a very good friend. We could easily introduce you . . . but only if you stay in Paris and model for me longer.

ISAKU: That is a very enticing offer. But I have a teaching post in Japan that I must return to. They are graciously letting me start in late September.

ANNETTE: What unfortunate timing.

ISAKU: As this may be the last time I see you, I hope that you, and Annette, will accept this gift.

(*ISAKU hands a gift box to ALBERTO. He opens it.*)

ALBERTO: This calligraphy set is exquisite.

ISAKU: I brought it from Japan. I was saving it for a special meeting here in Paris. I cannot envision a more special meeting . . . anywhere.

ANNETTE: Can you show us how to use it?

ISAKU: I am only an average calligrapher, I'm afraid. But I will gladly show you what I know . . . If only I had more time here.

ANNETTE: Why don't you stay a few more weeks?

ALBERTO: Or a few more months! Professor; my work is getting worse every day. At this rate, I will never finish another painting or sculpture. But if you stay and work with me, there is an opening for advancement like I have never made before. I will gladly pay to move you out of the Sorbonne housing and into a fine hotel on Boulevard Montparnasse. I will buy a new airline ticket to Japan and reimburse your current airfare. I will pay for all of your meals and drinks—whatever you need. You will not have any expenses whatsoever.

ISAKU: I'm flattered but—

ALBERTO:—I am not flattering you. I need you.

ANNETTE: Professor, please stay.

ISAKU: You are making it very hard to leave.

End of scene.

ACT I - Scene 3

ISAKU in his Meditation Room in Tokyo, 1966. He is draped in his mourning kimono.

ISAKU: Those first few sittings were the most excruciating physical challenge I ever had to endure. My back and neck ached like never before. At times, I thought I was losing sensation in my legs. But I never betrayed an iota of this to Alberto. I tried to sublimate this intense physical pain into a sublime meditative state. I knew that sitting for a maestro like Alberto was the opportunity of a lifetime and more. I longed to stay in Paris forever, sitting for the great artist every afternoon. And for three glorious summers, that's all I did.

> *(Transition to Alberto's studio, one year later, 1957.*
> *Sketches of Isaku now dominate the studio walls.*
> *ALBERTO sets up an easel. ISAKU enters.)*

ALBERTO: Professor, welcome back.

ISAKU: It's wonderful to be back. And what a gift to be liberated from student housing, thank you. But I must leave by August 15. I should start the semester on time this year.

ALBERTO: That will not be a problem, Professor.

ISAKU: Good. And please, call me Isaku.

ALBERTO: Very well, Isaku. Although I like being called "Maestro," please call me Alberto.

ISAKU: As you wish, Alberto. All last Autumn, you wouldn't allow me to pay for any cafés or restaurants. So, I brought you and Annette some of the finest sake from Japan.

ALBERTO: Thank you. Later, we will have to drink this together. Right now, please, sit right over there. As your time in Paris is very limited, I want to commit you to oil immediately.

> *(ISAKU sits in the model's chair, inches from the easel.)*

ISAKU: An inspired choice.

ALBERTO: Hopefully more inspired than these studies. Look at them—absolute trash. Cigarette?

ISAKU: No, thank you.

> *(ALBERTO lights a cigarette for himself and begins painting.)*

ALBERTO: Here we are: Eyes to me . . . Beautiful, hold that. Please move a little bit closer . . . Perfect. Words cannot convey what a joy it is to have you back in the studio.

ISAKU: To sit for you once was my greatest honor. To be invited back to your sacred studio . . . is more than I could ever ask for.

ALBERTO: After you left last fall, Jean Paul looked at the scraps from our sessions . . . he thought they were like nothing I have ever attempted before. He thinks if we keep working together, we can achieve true greatness. New greatness.

ISAKU: You showed Monsieur Sartre the scraps?

ALBERTO: Friends know to look in the trash bin to truly trace my progress . . . When the work is flowing, the studio is my sanctuary. When it's not flowing, every painting, every sculpture feels like a life and death struggle. Each stroke feels like my last breath . . . like one more feeble blow against the indomitable empire of death.

ISAKU: Is the dying Dutchman in every stroke?

ALBERTO: I moved to Paris a year after watching him die. I was still completely obsessed. I would walk the streets at night—running over every second of his last moments on Earth. . . One night I was walking past the Joan of Arc statue near the Tuileries. This car crashed right into me—knocking me straight up into the air! I never even remembered coming back down to Earth.

ISAKU: Alberto!

ALBERTO: When I finally came to; I was riding in the ambulance—face to face with the woman who drove the car. The woman who almost removed me from this earth . . . I just kept looking at her vile mouth and thinking how it would feel to violate her mouth—as a sculptor, of course—

ISAKU: Of course.

ALBERTO:—To plunge my palette knife between her vulgar lips, like thrusting a hook into a fish's mouth, and twisting it until those vulgar lips became beautiful again. The skin surrounding her lips would turn every shade of life and death—from bored to exuberant.

ISAKU: Perhaps you just wanted to kiss her?

ALBERTO: Maybe . . . I just needed to kiss her.

ISAKU: Why didn't you ask or just . . . steal a kiss?

ALBERTO: I just humbly receive what is coming to me. I had to use a cane for two years. My foot is still mangled. I am not as brave as my brother Diego who brazenly challenges fate. You have, no doubt, noticed Diego's severed fingers?

ISAKU: I have not, actually.

ALBERTO: His fingers were mangled in a childhood accident. Now he is so skilled and meticulous with those fingers. He makes my armatures and does most of the patinas. Now he's even designing his own furniture.

ISAKU: Losing something makes you take even greater care of what remains.

ALBERTO: I have a true artist by my side. Diego's severed fingers are my living sculpture—a daily reminder that I must fight to finish off the sculptures and paintings before they finish off me.

ISAKU: Your foot is also a living sculpture.

ALBERTO: My foot is just another mangled manifestation of fate. The driver's mouth, now that was a living sculpture. Even when I thought I would never walk again, I remember thinking what a perfect mouth to draw, to sculpt.

ISAKU: And to kiss. After what she did, I think you had a kiss coming to you.

ALBERTO: It was difficult to feel amorous after almost being killed at the foot of Joan of Arc.

ISAKU: Would you have been free of these inhibitions . . . at the Sphinx?

ALBERTO: If you are talking about The Sphinx being a place where one can indulge carnally without consequences—I do not subscribe to that notion.

Brothels are about intimacy without consequences.
Reinvention. Renewal.

ISAKU: Dare we call that… love?

ALBERTO:. . . Fate.

ISAKU: Perhaps that driver was your ambassador of
fate.

ALBERTO: No, just some drunken American who
would never respond to our insurance claims.

ISAKU: Americans don't know any bounds.

ALBERTO: The Americans may have liberated Europe,
but their cultural occupation is just beginning.

> *(ANNETTE enters. She is dressed elegantly for a night
> on the town.)*

ANNETTE: Alberto, please get ready for the concert.
Professor, so good to see you again.

ISAKU: And you.

ALBERTO: The professor's time with us is very limited.

ISAKU: We can start even earlier tomorrow. Please, do
what you must.

ALBERTO: Maybe we should drink some of that sake? The Professor brought us this exquisite sake.

ISAKU: A modest gift for such a prestigious honor.

ANNETTE: How lovely, but we need to go.

(DIEGO enters. He hands a telegram to ALBERTO, who reads it.)

DIEGO: Alberto, this just came in for us at Café Didot.

ALBERTO: Chase Manhattan wants to meet in London . . . the day after tomorrow? Diego, I am working with the professor now. I can't just up and leave.

DIEGO: This is a chance to have an outdoor sculpture in New York City.

ALBERTO: My work has been seen there for years.

DIEGO: Never like this. An outdoor sculpture will be permanent. Permanent. Your legacy in New York, America, and the world, will be assured.

ALBERTO: That's probably what they told Diego Rivera.

DIEGO: If you don't want to do this, just say so. Then Pierre would not have to keep their representatives at bay in New York, and I will not have to keep them at bay here at home . . .

ALBERTO: We wasted two days preparing for them last month. Then they didn't even show up.

DIEGO: They fly back to New York this weekend. We must meet with them.

ANNETTE: Professor, perhaps you would like to accompany me to the concert?

ISAKU: It would be my honor. But . . . . Maestro?

ALBERTO: Please, accompany Annette to the concert.

DIEGO: Then, it's settled. Let's go, Alberto.

ALBERTO: I'll just need a moment.

DIEGO: Alberto, let's telephone them from Café Didot. Immediately.

(ALBERTO furiously searches his studio.)

ALBERTO: Annette, where did we put that last payment from Pierre?

ANNETTE: We must open a bank account.

(ALBERTO pulls out wads of bills from hiding spots and hands them to ANNETTE.)

ALBERTO: This is for the next few days. Isaku, I need you to stay. Can you go home after the fifteenth?

ISAKU: Let me see what I can do.

ALBERTO: Be well, Annette. See you in a few days.

(All say goodbyes. DIEGO and ALBERTO exit.)

ANNETTE: Things are moving too quickly . . . Alberto is killing himself to keep up.

ISAKU: The Maestro seems more productive than ever.

ANNETTE: He's smoking and drinking much more than before. He doesn't let me take care of him. I've been trying to get us out of this squalor . . . Now that he can afford it, Alberto refuses to move.

ISAKU: Alberto can take better care of himself, and of you. But he needs to maintain this pace. It would be exciting to have his work in a public plaza in New York. Picasso hasn't even had such a distinction.

ANNETTE: Never mention Picasso. He always comes 'round the studio under the guise of seeking approval. But Alberto, like most artists in Paris, thinks Picasso is just keeping tabs on them.

ISAKU: I will make a note to never mention Picasso.

ANNETTE: Talk about New York instead . . . a permanent sculpture would be significant. I have always wanted to go there. Professor, have you been?

ISAKU: We of Japan are very leery of America.

ANNETTE: Excuse my insensitivity. Thank you for coming back to Paris. You don't know how much this is helping Alberto.

ISAKU: It is the Maestro and you who are changing my life.

ANNETTE: I . . . am changing your life?

ISAKU: The Maestro is allowing me to go from being an observer to a participant. His lovely wife is granting me admittance to the Maestro's intimate trinity.

ANNETTE: Well . . . thank you for such . . . acknowledgement . . . You're being here means so much to Alberto. Never have I heard such lively conversation while Alberto is working.

ISAKU: Your husband's focus is so strong. Like an undertow. You cannot help but get totally pulled in.

ANNETTE: That fascination usually goes one way. He is just as fascinated with you. Outside of Diego, you are the first male model to have this much impact on him. Alberto talks about you all the time.

ISAKU: Back in Japan, I could not stop thinking of sitting for him.

ANNETTE: Wait here a minute.

> *(ANNETTE exits into the adjoining room and returns with the calligraphy set and a pile of what looks like painted over newsprint. She spreads them out to show ISAKU.)*

ANNETTE: Alberto reads so many newspapers a day that I have started to use them for what I think of as studies for Japanese calligraphy. But they're just nonsensical characters.

ISAKU: Imaginary characters.

ANNETTE: Imaginary. That's a better way of expressing it.

ISAKU: Annette, these look inspired.

ANNETTE: I was inspired by your wonderful gift—thank you again, Professor.

ISAKU: Annette, please call me Isaku.

ANNETTE: Eeess . . .

ISAKU: EE-SA-KOO . . .

ANNETTE: Isaku. What a lovely name. Could you show me how to write my name in Japanese?

ISAKU: There's no exact translation. But why don't I show you the characters for . . . music.

ANNETTE: Wonderful, I do love music.

ISAKU: Let me show you . . . Line, point-point, turn! It's like a dance. Here, your turn. Hold the brush like this . . . Yes, very good! . . . Line . . .

ANNETTE: Line!

ISAKU: Point-point . . .

ANNETTE: Point-point!

ISAKU: Turn!

ANNETTE: Turn!

ISAKU: With no prior knowledge of Japanese, this is a great start.

ANNETTE: How do you pronounce these characters?

ISAKU: Ongaku.

ANNETTE: Ongggg . . .

ISAKU: Ga-

ANNETTE: Ga

ISAKU: Ku. On-ga-ku.

ANNETTE: On-ga-ku. Written or spoken, the Japanese language is so beautiful. It's like music itself.

ISAKU: Music, like great art, goes beyond language and cuts right to the core. Art and music; I could not imagine life without them.

ANNETTE: Is there an exact translation for Isaku?

ISAKU: Yes, but not in Japanese. Isaku comes from the biblical "Isaac." Father was a devout Catholic. He led a movement to choose Jesus over Emperor. I could not accept his God. I could not accept any God. There is only the self. I chose a life of Philosophy. French Existential philosophy.

ANNETTE: I also broke with my family to come here. I met Alberto at a French Resistance meeting in Geneva. I was stationed there as a secretary for the International Red Cross. After the war my contract ran out, so I followed Alberto to Paris. My family is very bourgeois— my father was a schoolmaster—so they did not approve of my coming here to be with Alberto.

ISAKU: You made the right choice.

ANNETTE: I'd like to think so. Oh, it's almost time for the concert. Thank you again for accompanying me.

ISAKU: It is my honor. I just wish I had worn better attire. Your outfit looks stunning.

ANNETTE: I'm so glad you like it. I have to admit; it's from Patricia, Pierre's wife.

ISAKU: So, this is modern style?

ANNETTE: Yes, but from last year. Every year Patricia gives me her formal outfits from last season. Simone, Jean Paul's companion, does the same thing.

ISAKU: Dresses from Patricia Matisse and Simone de Beauvoir, two of the most remarkable women in Paris. This must please Alberto.

ANNETTE: It may please Alberto. But what would please Annette is if Alberto himself would buy me some new dresses.

ISAKU: He will, Annette, he will.

ANNETTE: Shall we go?

ISAKU: The night is calling.

End of scene.

ACT I - Scene 4

Café Didot later that night. ALBERTO is drinking wine and reading from newspapers spread out on a table in front of him. Suitcases are at his feet. DIEGO enters.

DIEGO: Chase Manhattan sent another telegram. Two train tickets await us, and they'll meet us at the other end.

ALBERTO: We can't go.

DIEGO: Alberto, please—

ALBERTO:—Have you read the papers? Somehow America, maybe even Chase Manhattan, has something to do with this Suez fiasco. With all the time de Gaulle spent in London, you would think he could stand up to them.

DIEGO: Our task in London is considerably less daunting.

ALBERTO: Then let's go.

DIEGO: Maybe the Suez crisis calls for a sharing of power?

ALBERTO: Power can never be shared.

DIEGO: It can, but only if all of the parties involved really want it.

ALBERTO: Does anyone ever really want to share power?

DIEGO: You'd be surprised.

(They drink wine and read newspapers in silence for a few beats.)

DIEGO: They keep talking about a tunnel between France and Great Britain.

ALBERTO: It will never happen.

DIEGO: But just imagine, a tunnel beneath the English Channel.

ALBERTO: Imagine all you want. It will never happen.

DIEGO: But if it did . . . there would be a permanent link.

ALBERTO: There will never be a permanent link between England and France.

DIEGO: Until then, we'll just have to be content with trains running over land and ships sailing on the sea. We're taking the overnight train, so we can relax.

ALBERTO: Time for another bottle of wine.

DIEGO: You're drinking much more than usual.

ALBERTO: I'm worried about what's going on.

DIEGO: The world is in a precarious state, but that's nothing new.

ALBERTO: Yes, the world is in a precarious state. But so is the studio.

DIEGO: What's wrong in the studio?

ALBERTO: I have never faced an obstacle like drawing the Professor. I just cannot seem to capture his likeness. It's like a language I cannot learn or a country I cannot conquer.

DIEGO: Alberto, a head is just a head. Move forward.

ALBERTO: Backwards seems to be my direction lately.

DIEGO: Pierre also sent a telegram.

ALBERTO: Checking up to make sure we get on the train?

DIEGO: He has invited me to submit a proposal to design his next gallery in New York.

ALBERTO: Magnificent! I'm sure you'll get the commission.

DIEGO: A trip to New York is a must, and very soon.

ALBERTO: Diego, we have plenty to do right here in Paris. And now you'll be designing Pierre's gallery . . . I don't see how we can go to New York.

DIEGO: At least we're finally meeting with the Chase Manhattan people.

ALBERTO: If they show up.

DIEGO: Everything's going to be fine.

ALBERTO: We'll see.

> *(They continue to drink wine and read newspapers in silence. End of scene.)*

ACT I - Scene 5

The studio even later that night. ISAKU walks ANNETTE home after the concert.

ANNETTE: It's a little stuffy in here, but would you like stay for a drink?

ISAKU: Why don't we go to Café Didot?

ANNETTE: I've been there twice already today. The third time will not be a charm. Believe me.

ISAKU: I really should go. But first, I bought one of their recordings tonight as a present for you and Alberto.

ANNETTE: You're the guest, yet you're showering us with gifts.

ISAKU: You and the Maestro treated me to so many magnificent restaurants and cafes last Autumn.

ANNETTE: But you were the gentleman who walked me home while Alberto would disappear into the Montparnasse night. Let's listen to the recording. We have a phonograph in the next room.

ISAKU: I wouldn't want to inconvenience you.

ANNETTE: We can drink some of that wonderful Sake you gave us.

ISAKU: Shouldn't we wait for the Maestro?

ANNETTE: You're probably right . . . we have some wine. Would you care for some?

ISAKU: I can never resist French wine.

ANNETTE: Great, we'll have some wine and listen to the recording.

ISAKU: I'll pour the wine.

> *(ANNETTE exits into the adjoining bedroom with the 78 recording. ISAKU takes the cork out of a half-drunken bottle of wine, wipes off two glasses and fills them up. We hear Gospel music. ANNETTE re-enters. ISAKU hands her a glass of wine.)*

ANNETTE: Some On-Ga-Ku.

ISAKU: Inspiring Ongaku. To Paris: The "City of Lights," art and life!

ANNETTE: To you being here with us!

> *(They lift their glasses, toast and drink.)*

ANNETTE: Wasn't the concert just extraordinary?

ISAKU: I have never seen or heard anything like the Fisk Jubilee Singers.

ANNETTE: With this phonograph record, at least Alberto will be able to hear this . . . powerful music. It's like African spirituals . . . but they're singing in English. This combination is very powerful, but very bizarre. In America they call this music, Gospel.

ISAKU: As in The Bible?

ANNETTE: No, as in the church choir. America has given Paris: Miss Josephine Baker; Mister Man Ray and tonight, the Fisk Jubilee Singers. I wonder what it's like to live in America with so many different kinds of people all living side by side.

ISAKU: It must be like Paris. I am from Japan. You, the Maestro and Diego are from Switzerland.

(The Gospel music goes silent.)

ANNETTE: This record is lovely, but let's play side two another time.

(ANNETTE exits into the adjoining bedroom. We hear bebop jazz. ANNETTE re-enters.)

ANNETTE: I only play these recordings when Alberto isn't working. We both love classical music, but I still love American be-bop. We listened to be-bop all the time back in Geneva. Do you like be-bop?

ISAKU: Secretly, I do. But I could never tell my university colleagues in Japan.

ANNETTE: You can be yourself in Paris . . .

ISAKU: I'm coming around to that conclusion.

ANNETTE: When you sit for Alberto; do you ever wonder what it would be like to trade places with him?

ISAKU: I have not actually.

ANNETTE: At first, I didn't either. Now I get extremely jealous. Just imagine I'm Alberto. When he picks up his brush, it's like being at the symphony just as the conductor raises his baton. There's nothing in the world like those first few seconds. Each one of your senses, every fiber of your being is as alert and alive as it will ever be. You start feeling lightheaded from the flood of adrenaline pumping into every pore of your body. I just want to leap out of my seat and scream, "Alberto, put the brush down and dance with me."

ISAKU: But you are both . . . dancing.

ANNETTE: He's dancing. You and I are sitting— perfectly still, for hours. It's not fair that only Alberto gets to absorb, gets to devour, gets to feast on that amazing sensation that takes over the room. The model should get that chance too. Wouldn't you agree?

ISAKU: Honestly, I have never contemplated the process in that context.

ANNETTE: Then let me rephrase myself, would you like to dance?

ISAKU: I would love to.

ANNETTE: Some more wine?

ISAKU: I would love that too.

ANNETTE: Let me pour . . . We're getting towards the end of the bottle.

ISAKU: Then let us start on the Sake.

ANNETTE: Are you sure?

ISAKU: Absolutely.

(ISAKU & ANNETTE begin to dance.)

ANNETTE: I do hope you can stay in Paris a little longer.

ISAKU: Let us follow the ongaku . . .

(They dance a few beats, the music ends.)

ISAKU: Side two?

ANNETTE: Yes. But shall we play it in your hotel room? The phonograph is portable.

ISAKU: Are you sure?

ANNETTE: Absolutely . . . Let me pack up the phonograph.

> *(ANNETTE exits. ALBERTO enters, carrying his suitcase.)*

ISAKU: Maestro, I am sorry to be here so late.

ALBERTO: Not a problem.

> *(ANNETTE enters, carrying the phonograph.)*

ALBERTO: Annette, Chase Manhattan cancelled again. I just want to drop off my suitcase and pick up some notes. I'm going back to Café Didot to write some letters.

ANNETTE: You can write here if you like. Isaku and I are going out.

ALBERTO: No, I prefer to write in the café. Isaku, are you free to work tomorrow afternoon?

ISAKU: Yes, I would love to.

ALBERTO: Grand. You two have a wonderful evening.

ISAKU: See you . . . tomorrow?

ALBERTO: Maybe I will finally be able to see you tomorrow. Annette, you will bring back the phonograph?

ANNETTE: Of course, I will. Good night, Alberto.

(ANNETTE and ISAKU exit. ALBERTO is alone in his studio. End of Scene.)

ACT I - Scene 6

The studio the next day. The heretofore random black, gray and white sketches on the walls are now a series of studies of ISAKU's face. ALBERTO is setting up an easel. ISAKU enters.

ISAKU: Thank you for starting a few hours later.

ALBERTO: You're a lifeline.

ISAKU: I am just your witness . . . Alberto, about last night . . .

ALBERTO: Is this about Annette spending the night at your hotel?

ISAKU: Well . . . uhm . . .

ALBERTO: If Annette had spent the night with a less enlightened being, then I would object. The parameters of marriage, like all conventions, must be expanded. Shall we?

ISAKU: Without delay.

   (ALBERTO begins painting.)

ALBERTO: Look at me . . . Directly at me . . . Stare right through me . . . Beautiful, hold that . . . Before New York disrupted me again, I was just starting to find your beautiful face on this canvas.

ISAKU: May you find it again . . . Maybe today I can take a look?

ALBERTO: Not yet. Let us continue.

(ALBERTO resumes painting. Time passes . . . he abruptly stops.)

ALBERTO: This is still not working!

ISAKU: Please, let me take a look.

ALBERTO: All right.

ISAKU: Alberto, this is a strong beginning.

ALBERTO: It's all wrong!

(ALBERTO destroys the canvas.)

ISAKU: A foundation was there.

ALBERTO: It's hard to explain, but I need to paint you out in order to paint you in . . . Right now, I only seem to be able to paint you in, but not out. Can you work a little longer today?

ISAKU: Of course. . . But we're losing light.

ALBERTO: We can work by electric light . . . Cigarette?

ISAKU: Yes.

ALBERTO: Yes?

ISAKU: Yes.

ALBERTO: I'll light our cigarettes. Then we'll light up this night.

> *(ALBERTO, pleasantly surprised, places a cigarette in ISAKUs mouth, lights it up. He lights one up for himself then sets up the electric light.)*

ISAKU: I will enjoy working at night. I have always found the night to be magical.

ALBERTO: I love the night, but I've always feared the dark. The night the Dutchman died I turned on every light in my hotel room. I didn't dare go to sleep. I feared I would be joining my departed traveling companion. I have slept with the light on every night since. It drives Annette crazy.

ISAKU: We will work at night but stay out of the darkness.

ALBERTO: I just need a different canvas for electric light . . . Diego has only prepared one canvas today . . . I can paint over yesterday's canvas . . .

> *(ALBERTO rummages around and finds a canvas with ANNETTE's face on it. ISAKU sees it and has a strong reaction. ALBERTO resumes painting.)*

ALBERTO: Here we are: Show me your eyes . . . Just like that . . . Lovely.

ISAKU: If you cannot see someone on the canvas . . . they no longer exist for you?

ALBERTO: Are you falling in love with her? . . . It would be fine with me . . .

ISAKU: Maestro—

ALBERTO: Alberto, please.

ISAKU: Alberto, I don't . . . no. I am not falling in love. Must you paint my image over Annette's?

ALBERTO: Into Annette. Not over Annette. This is just a study of "Annette" It is not Annette . . . Can you please turn your head?

ISAKU: You only want to paint half of my face?

ALBERTO: I want to paint a different side of you.

ISAKU: Shall I turn this way?

ALBERTO: No, the other way . . . that's it. Yes, Isaku. Yes . . . I . . . have never painted Annette or even Diego in profile . . . Only you, Isaku. . . There is only you . . .

ISAKU: I wish we could stay this way forever.

ALBERTO: Nothing . . . nothing in the world . . . comes close to this . . . Nothing. You're a Godsend.

ISAKU: Not from God. Just from Japan.

ALBERTO: Damn it! I can't see you anymore.

ISAKU: I am right here.

ALBERTO: I had you right here. In my mind, in my eye and finally in my hands. Now, I've lost you forever.

ISAKU: Alberto, look at me. See me.

ALBERTO: Straight on or in profile . . . I can't seem to paint you in or out. When I was a child, father was always going away for painting exhibitions. I would become petrified with anxiety. Once it got so bad that I could not remember his face.

ISAKU: How did you come out of that?

ALBERTO: Diego explained father's face—detail by detail. That never happened again . . . until just now.

ISAKU: Should I turn my head back?

ALBERTO: Yes, but slowly. Very slowly . . . NOOOO! Stop! Who are you?

ISAKU: It is only me, Isaku.

ALBERTO: Don't destroy me.

ISAKU: Stay out of the darkness, Alberto.

ALBERTO: I'm sorry. I am so sorry.

ISAKU: We are here to neither destroy nor control.

ALBERTO: Isaku, I need you to stay. My life depends on it. My eyes have deserted me. My hands have deserted me. Please don't leave me.

ISAKU: Give me your hand.

ALBERTO: If you lose your teaching position, I will support you and your family. I swear.

ISAKU: It's not that—

ALBERTO:—You can find another university. If I cannot paint your face it will be the end of my existence. Let's work some more.

ISAKU: Alberto, there will be time for that later. For now, just give me your hand and rest.

> (ALBERTO offers his hand. ISAKU embraces ALBERTO.)

ALBERTO: Then you will stay in Paris longer?

ISAKU: I am here for you, Alberto

ALBERTO: I can't be abandoned anymore.

ISAKU: There is nothing left but to carry on.

ALBERTO: Come with me to the brothels tonight. I will pay for you . . . Going to the brothels together will make our bond complete . . . Intimacy without consequences. Reinvention. Renewal.

ISAKU: Our bond is already complete. Just focus on the work.

ALBERTO: We should only work at night.

End of Scene.

ACT I - Scene 7

DIEGO is in the studio working with his lamps and candelabras.
On a wall, sketches of ISAKU hover over the scene like ghosts.
ANNETTE enters.

ANNETTE: I'm going to Café Didot. Care to join me?

DIEGO: I can't, thanks. Before you go, can you help me set-up? A photographer is coming in two hours,

ANNETTE: Of course. I had no idea Alberto was hiring a photographer.

(They begin moving things around the studio.)

DIEGO: I hired the photographer. Let's move these lights first. Pierre wants to see more of my work before making final decisions. With Pierre having an even stronger New York presence, I think Alberto is letting the opportunity of a lifetime slip through his fingers.

ANNETTE: Alberto thinks they really want Calder.

DIEGO: I wish he'd spend more time on the New York studies and less on the Professor. Look at these sketches. They don't even look like they came from Alberto's hand.

ANNETTE: He's on the verge of a big breakthrough with Isaku.

DIEGO: Only Alberto knows where this is going. But so far, I think his work with Isaku is taking him backwards . . . artistically and personally.

ANNETTE: Alberto would never say this, but your designing Pierre's gallery is becoming a huge distraction.

DIEGO: And your carrying on with the Professor is not?

ANNETTE: While I lie awake, alone in our bed with the light on. Alberto is at a different brothel every night.

DIEGO: He revealed everything to you in Geneva.

ANNETTE: As a brother, you couldn't be more loyal or supportive. You tend to all of the details that Alberto doesn't like to do—

DIEGO:—excuse me, Annette. All of the things I do for his sculptures are not things that he doesn't want to do. Those are all things that Alberto cannot do.

ANNETTE: Are we finished here?

DIEGO: Do you think Alberto would mind if we moved his easel into the corner?

ANNETTE: Only if it's temporary.

> (*As they move the easel, DIEGO discovers a stored painting that startles him.*)

DIEGO: Oh my God. Look at this . . .

ANNETTE:. . . I have never seen Alberto use this kind of under painting . . .

DIEGO: That's not under painting . . . Look carefully . . . He's painted the Professor over you.

ANNETTE: Alberto would never do that.

DIEGO: Look again.

End of scene.

ACT I - Scene 8

The studio the following month. DIEGO enters carrying a large box. He turns the studio lights on to reveal ALBERTO who appears to be working in the dark. There are now assorted lamps and candelabras among the works-in-progress in the cramped studio.

DIEGO: Alberto! Have you slept at all?

ALBERTO: Couldn't. I need to work. Would you mind sitting?

DIEGO: Why don't you go to sleep now? I have to work on my proposal for Pierre.

ALBERTO: Just a drawing . . . please.

DIEGO: Perhaps we can focus on the New York studies? The plaza scale model arrived this morning.

ALBERTO: New York can wait. We need to work right here, right now.

DIEGO: We've worked so hard for this opportunity. Let's put more time towards it.

ALBERTO: Do they know that I have never worked on that large a scale? Do they know that I have a fear of heights? The buildings in the plaza will be sixty stories high. There's not a building that tall in all of Paris.

DIEGO: Your sculptures will still be on the ground and you must adjust.

ALBERTO: For scale and perspective, I always return to Rembrandt's "Landscape with Three Trees." The human figures in that etching are dwarfed by nature, not manmade creations. I'm not sure I understand New York. But I'm also on bad terms with Rembrandt. I went to The Louvre last week and we couldn't communicate. I must get back to my portraits of Isaku.

DIEGO: You have always wanted an outdoor sculpture in a prominent place. New York will be the new capital of the world. Your sculptures will be the sentry and entry point. But instead you're focusing on the Professor.

ALBERTO: Even if we accept that commission, we won't even be able to assemble the final work here.

DIEGO: Perhaps we need a larger studio.

ALBERTO: The studio was big enough before you got the commission from Pierre.

DIEGO: I do not have the commission, Alberto, I am just submitting a proposal.

ALBERTO: Why are your lamps out?

DIEGO: I need to send a few studies to Pierre. Are they taking up too much room?

ALBERTO: Diego, this is our studio.

DIEGO: Alberto, this is your studio.

ALBERTO: You spend just as much time in it as I do.

DIEGO: Primarily to work on your pieces.

ALBERTO: I have always encouraged you to develop your own work.

DIEGO: Only in so far as it does not get in the way of your work.

ALBERTO: Diego, this is our work. I could not do this without you.

DIEGO: In the studio, that's understood. Beyond this room, nobody knows me.

ALBERTO: Fate has granted you this big New York commission.

DIEGO: Alberto, my lamps may be hanging from the ceiling of Pierre's new gallery, but they will be shining light onto your sculptures and paintings.

ALBERTO: May we at least try to get back to work?

> *(DIEGO sits in the model seat. ALBERTO moves from his clay station to pick up his drawing pad, but first has to move a few lamps. He begins drawing.)*

ALBERTO: Here we are, show me your eyes. Please hold that . . . Lovely . . . Lovely . . . This is flowing. Please don't move, Isaku.

DIEGO: Alberto! It's me, Diego.

ALBERTO: Pardon . . . Just a momentary lapse. Have you put on weight?

DIEGO: Not since last night.

ALBERTO: Have your eyes always been this round?

DIEGO: Only when I open them— Alberto, why are you talking like this?

ALBERTO: Just having trouble getting started.

DIEGO: We should really go to Café Didot.

ALBERTO: I don't need coffee. I just need to work. Please, be still.

DIEGO: Alberto, I have not moved.

ALBERTO: Diego, I cannot see! Remember when we were kids and I could not remember Father's face? I am having that anxiety again. I need to see Isaku. Not just in my memory, but straight in front of me.

DIEGO: The Professor? After two consecutive summers, I thought you were finished with him.

ALBERTO: I thought so, too. But I still feel there is an opening for advancement like I have never known before.

DIEGO: What about his advancement with Annette?

ALBERTO: Isaku makes her happy. I want Annette to be happy.

DIEGO: His affair with Annette is having an adverse effect on your work.

ALBERTO: How could Annette being happy possibly have any negative effect on my work?

DIEGO: Are you happy with the work so far?

ALBERTO: It's dreadful. But without failure, there can be no success.

DIEGO: At a certain point, you have to cut your losses.

ALBERTO: I can only stay the course.

DIEGO: You can be more faithful.

ALBERTO: Faithful?

DIEGO: Faithful.

ALBERTO: Faithful . . . to Annette?

DIEGO: Faithful . . . to me!

ALBERTO: You're jealous.

DIEGO: Me? Jealous of the Professor? Be serious, Alberto.

ALBERTO: When he's here, you never sit for me.

DIEGO: Alberto, I think you're jealous of the Professor.

ALBERTO: Absurd. If I were jealous of Isaku, why would I keep bringing him back to Paris—at great expense, I might add.

DIEGO: If you lose the Professor, you will lose Annette. Forever.

ALBERTO: Nonsense.

DIEGO: If you cannot confront the Professor, you must confront yourself.

(ALBERTO abruptly stops drawing.)

ALBERTO: It's impossible to work here. Let's take a break.

DIEGO: If you'll excuse me, I have to get to work.

(DIEGO exits. ANNETTE enters and sits in the model seat vacated by DIEGO. ALBERTO resumes drawing.)

ALBERTO: Diego, where were we?

ANNETTE: Alberto, It's me, Annette.

ALBERTO: Yes, of course. Everything seems bigger, inflated somehow, like your nose.

ANNETTE: My nose?

ALBERTO: Yes, your nose. It seems larger today.

ANNETTE: I am not Pinocchio.

ALBERTO: And I am not Gepetto.

ANNETTE: Alberto, do you need to take a rest?

ALBERTO: Annette!. . . You've never asked me that before . . . I'm fine. Let's continue. Let me see your eyes . . . A little higher . . . That's fine . . . Don't move.

ANNETTE: I am not moving.

ALBERTO: Please, don't move!

ANNETTE: I AM NOT MOVING! I'm sorry. It's just . . . The studio is as small as our hotel room in Geneva. Alberto, we've outgrown this space. Just look at you. You're wound-up so tightly like you're about to implode. We need room to grow. I rented the room next door the moment it became available. Then at least we had a place to sleep outside of the studio.

ALBERTO: I supported you on that.

ANNETTE: You paid for it, yes. But I did the renovation while you and Diego kept working in here. Alberto, we need more space and we can afford it. We don't need a bourgeois palace or a chateau in Provence, just another room or two.

ALBERTO: My work won't sell forever.

ANNETTE: Open a bank account. Save something, Alberto.

ALBERTO: I am at a critical juncture . . . any change would be devastating . . . I can rent you a room next door to Isaku every time he comes back to Paris.

ANNETTE: Is this about Isaku?

ALBERTO: This is about me. I can't see you. I can't see Diego or Isaku—in my eyes or my mind.

ANNETTE: I wish Isaku never had to leave.

ALBERTO: We must invite him back next summer. I need to finish my work with him.

ANNETTE: I want to have his child.

(ALBERTO abruptly stops drawing.)

ALBERTO: Strange, I had a dream that you and Isaku had a child. But this child bore no resemblance to any of us. I could not even tell if it was a boy or a girl.

ANNETTE: Did you still love this child?

ALBERTO: Annette, why now?

ANNETTE: In Geneva, you told me your limitations. I accepted them because we had each other. Here in Paris, I feel like I don't have you anymore. For too many years I slept alone in that tiny bedroom with the light on, while you would go to Boulevard Montparnasse until dawn. Alberto, if you won't sleep in our bed anymore, I want to sleep in a different bed. A bed where there is more than just a flimsy wall separating our marriage from all of the dust, fumes and energy of this studio. I will still take care of you and the studio every day. But I cannot live here anymore.

ALBERTO: I will buy a new apartment. Choose any one that I can afford. But you will live there, not me.

ANNETTE: It will not be much different.

ALBERTO: You never spoke this way before Isaku.

ANNETTE: You will always be my husband. But you have your art. I don't even have my family name. I want to give something, contribute something to the future. I want my own legacy.

ALBERTO: My legacy is our legacy. But this child would be the legacy of you and Isaku. Annette, I have encouraged you to have a child with any number of my friends.

ANNETTE: How would this be any different than having a child with Pierre or Aime?

ALBERTO: I don't know. It just would . . . Shall we get back to work?

ANNETTE: I think you need to rest.

ALBERTO: I really need to work . . . Here we are: Eyes to me . . . Perfect. Please hold that, Isaku.

ANNETTE: Alberto!

ALBERTO: Isaku, I can't hear you.

ANNETTE: It's me, Annette!

ALBERTO: I still can't hear you. Isaku.

ANNETTE: Aaaahhhhhh . . .

(ANNETTE makes a primal non-verbal vocal sound that grows to a loud crescendo. ALBERTO keeps drawing.)

ALBERTO: ISAKU? . . . ISAKU?

End of ACT I. Intermission optional.

ACT II - Scene 1

Tokyo, January 11, 1966. ISAKU sits in his Meditation Room before a bust that bears his likeness. He is draped in a mourning kimono.

ISAKU: The first time I saw the Maestro's work, it was the dead of winter—my first winter in Paris. I didn't know a soul there. I didn't know a street there. I was never more isolated. The Maestro's work consoled me like no other human being ever could . . . or ever will. I never dreamed I would get the chance to enter the world of that work . . . to enter the great artist's life and mind. My final sitting for the Maestro was during the autumn after Father died. My family no longer felt like family. Tokyo no longer felt like home. All I had left was the man who would give me my eternal essence. One can always go back, but you don't always resume where you left off.

> *(As in the Prologue, ISAKU's Meditation Room transforms into ALBERTO's studio. It is 1959, nighttime. When the transition is complete, ISAKU rises, removes his mourning kimono to reveal a 1950s style tweed western business suit.)*

ISAKU: Alberto?. . . Are you here? Alberto???

> *(ISAKU finds a half-drunken bottle of wine and pours himself a glass. DIEGO enters.)*

DIEGO: Professor, you're here so late?

ISAKU: Alberto only wants to work at night now.
Would you care to join me for some wine?

DIEGO: No, thanks. But you please enjoy, Professor.

ISAKU: Diego, please, call me Isaku . . . *(DIEGO does not
reply.)* While my country works diligently to lift herself out
of a hangover of defeat, I sit here in Paris drinking wine.
What a peculiar world this place is. What a peculiar state
that peace is.

DIEGO: Peace is important, in the home as well as on
the field of battle.

ISAKU: This candelabra is quite striking. It's very
unusual for Alberto.

DIEGO: It's not Alberto's. It's mine.

ISAKU: Your artist's voice is very strong in this piece.

DIEGO: Thank you, Professor, but the art stands on its
own. Art is never about the people making it and
certainly not about the people buying it. Art should only
exist and stand for the art itself.

ISAKU: How long have you been making work like this?

DIEGO: Back in Switzerland I had an apprenticeship
with a cemetery engraver. Designing candelabrum and

other interior pieces is how Alberto and I survived after we first arrived.

ISAKU: You moved to Paris together?

DIEGO: Alberto was here first. Our first flat was right across from the Montparnasse cemetery. Some nights you could still see vapors rising from the decomposing corpses.

ISAKU: Alberto is fortunate to have an older brother to look out for him.

DIEGO: Professor, I'm the younger brother.

ISAKU: Yet you are the more protective, the more practical one.

DIEGO: Sometimes, too practical.

ISAKU: Can one be "too practical?"

DIEGO: As a child, I never liked the look of my fingers. Back in Stampa during the height of summer, all of us boys would work in the fields gathering straw. I helped with this as soon as I was able—I think I was no more than four. The older boys would operate these massive machines that would grind the straw down for horse feed. One day when the older boys weren't paying attention, I stuck my fingers right into the machine. "Are you crazy? Do you want to die?"—the older boys started screaming. As they tore me away from the machine, I didn't even look up at them. I just kept watching my blood and cartilage spurting all over—staining the golden straw a dirty crimson.

ISAKU: Alberto thought you had mangled your fingers in an accident.

DIEGO: There are no accidents, Professor. Including my being here in Paris. You might not see it now, but I owe a lot to Alberto. Since childhood, we've always been so different, yet we've built a world together.

ISAKU: The world is composed of disparate parts.

DIEGO: Human chemistry is a mystery.

ISAKU: Much like The Sphinx.

DIEGO: We can all learn a lot from the Sphinx.

ISAKU: Has Alberto taken you there?

DIEGO: Professor, I traveled to Algeria and Egypt on my own.

ISAKU: I was referring to—

DIEGO:—I know what you were referring to . . .

(ALBERTO enters.)

ISAKU: Alberto!

ALBERTO: Isaku, welcome back!

(The new studio telephone rings.)

ISAKU: A telephone?

ALBERTO: Unfortunately.

DIEGO: I'll get it.

(DIEGO exits.)

ALBERTO: I'm afraid that telephones have become a necessary evil.

ISAKU: Evil, yes. Necessary, I'm not so sure.

(DIEGO enters.)

DIEGO: Some American wants to speak to "His eminence, Monsieur Giacometti."

ALBERTO: Isaku is here. I can't speak to him now.

DIEGO: Very well. But why don't you tell him?

ALBERTO: Excuse us.

(ALBERTO and DIEGO exit.)

ISAKU: How I have missed this place.

(ISAKU kisses the studio floor and takes out a camera from his coat and starts taking photographs. ALBERTO enters.)

ALBERTO: Here we are—you brought a camera?

ISAKU: Is it all right . . .?

ALBERTO: Please, but only take a few.

(ISAKU resumes taking photographs.)

ISAKU: Sounds like you just had a very important telephone call.

ALBERTO: Apparently Diego was the "eminent Monsieur Giacometti" the American wished to speak to. His handiwork is becoming quite renowned . . . Can we get to work?

(ISAKU puts camera away.)

ISAKU: Sorry, Alberto. I didn't see your set-up.

ALBERTO: I thought we'd go right to clay. Would you like some boiled eggs or cheese with your wine?

ISAKU: Are we going to Café Didot?

ALBERTO: No, we can eat right here. Annette leaves a basket of food before she goes home.

ISAKU: Home?

ALBERTO: Yes, I bought her an apartment on the rue Leopold-Robert, about five-minutes-walk from here . . . she didn't tell you?

ISAKU: Are you two . . .

ALBERTO: We're still married. Annette comes by every day. Do you remember your pose from last time?

ISAKU: Yes!

> *(They sit knee to knee. ISAKU settles in, ALBERTO*
> *starts sculpting. Time passes.)*

ALBERTO: Your muscle memory is astounding.

ISAKU: Every day in Japan, I would meditate and imagine that I was right back here, sitting for you— doing what I love to do most in this world.

ALBERTO: Memory: The well of life—

ISAKU:—and the well of art.

ALBERTO: With your camera, do you seek tangible proof of our intangible process?

ISAKU: In photography, the image never touches human hands. That is an intangible process. Your hands, your fingers are shaping the clay. That is a tangible process.

ALBERTO: The clay may be in my hands, but the image is not . . . maybe I should buy a camera.

ISAKU: Before father died, I did not even own a camera . . . Since father died, everything's a blur. I could not go back to teaching . . . Thank you for inviting me back.

ALBERTO: I am always here for you. What was your father like?

ISAKU: Father was a very brave man. Some say, a very stupid man.

ALBERTO: Calling someone stupid is the inept retort of a vapid soul.

ISAKU: Those souls were in the majority among father's university colleagues. Father spoke out against Japan's occupation of China. A barbaric witch-hunt banned him and his writings. He was removed swiftly. He wanted me to restore the family honor by pursuing medicine—like his father and his father's father. When I chose a life of Philosophy, father stopped encouraging me.

ALBERTO: My father, Giovanni, was a painter. He encouraged me as a child. But later, he, and my mother, vehemently disapproved of my artistic choices . . . Pleasing one's parents can be a thankless task. Pierre

Matisse, my New York dealer, is the son of Henri. He understands this more than most.

ISAKU: Alberto, may I take a photograph of you while you're working?

ALBERTO: Memory is more faithful to reality than photos. But go ahead . . . Cigarette?

> *(ISAKU takes photographs. ALBERTO lights up the first of a succession of cigarettes.)*

ISAKU: Later. Photos are merely an elixir for memory. Not a replacement for memory.

> *(ISAKU puts his camera away and settles into his pose. ALBERTO resumes working.)*

ALBERTO: O.K. Eyes to me . . . just like that . . .
Nature was once my muse, my mistress and my witness. Not anymore. Annette tells me that she wants to have a child with you.

ISAKU: It is she who made that request.

ALBERTO: At first, I objected. I used to think that you and Annette having a child would be a distraction and detriment to our making art, making legacy. Now, I think it's a good idea. Nature took procreation out of my hands as a very young man. How old are you?

ISAKU: I am Forty.

ALBERTO: I am fifty-nine, almost as old as the Dutchman when he died in front of my eyes. You and I are reliving that relationship . . . only this time, I am the Dutchman and I will be the one who dies.

ISAKU: Stay out of the darkness, Alberto—

ALBERTO: When I die my spirit will flow right into you. Isaku, have that child with Annette.

ISAKU: Remain in light.

ALBERTO: The work we are creating here is our offspring, Isaku. This is the legacy of you and me. The child you create with Annette will be the offspring, the legacy, for all three of us.

ISAKU: Alberto, perhaps we should take a rest—

ALBERTO:—Are you getting tired?

ISAKU: No, I'm happy to keep working.

ALBERTO: Then let's continue . . . When the Dutchman died I was reciting from Flaubert's "Bouvard et Petuchet." That book is on my shelf in the bedroom. Go find it. Now!

ISAKU: We should take a rest—

ALBERTO: —No, let's keep working! Even though it won't help . . . Every time I look at you . . . I see Annette. I should just stop working altogether. Let's make a trade: my studio for your camera.

ISAKU: I don't follow . . .

ALBERTO: Just give me your camera and this studio will be yours. Diego will support you and Annette is already under your spell

ISAKU: Annette is not "under my spell" or under any spell.

ALBERTO: Then why do I see her face when I look at yours?

ISAKU: Alberto. . . Let's stop working on this piece and start anew.

ALBERTO: We can stop working on this piece, but we can never start anew . . . I will try one final time. But we must make a pact. And you must keep your word no matter what—can I count on you? *(Pause)* Can I count on you?

ISAKU: Yes.

ALBERTO: We must perform some alchemy here . . . The only way out of this void is to have both you and Annette pose for me at the same time. Turn this aberration into gold.

ISAKU: Excellent solution.

ALBERTO: Only if I succeed. If I cannot . . . you must help me commit hara-kiri.

ISAKU: Alberto?

ALBERTO: I couldn't save the Dutchman. Let me see if I can save myself.

End of Scene.

ACT II / Scene 2

The studio the next day. ANNETTE & ISAKU sit. ALBERTO,
behind an easel, is painting them.

ALBERTO: This is lovely. Eyes up, Annette. To me.
Excellent. Eyes up, Isaku, great. Please hold that. We
should have done this sooner . . . So much sooner . . .
We . . . We can never make up for lost time . . . But we
can find it in our minds.

> *(ALBERTO continues to paint feverishly, making feral*
> *vocal sounds as he works. ANNETTE has an internal*
> *moment.)*

ANNETTE: That tiny bedroom always felt like a coffin.
As I slept alone with the light on, I felt like a young
widow whose husband was living but was just dead to
her. Today, the whole studio feels like a cemetery. We sit
here, waiting for Alberto to make us come alive again.

ALBERTO: I still can't tell you two apart. Let's try a
different pose . . . Double profile—please face each
other. And stand. Move a little bit closer . . . Fine. Now
lock eyes . . . Deeply . . . Intimately . . . Yes. Please hold
that . . . This is rare . . . I can actually see what is in front
of me. I am no longer trapped in The Academy. I am
alive here. Today.

> *(ALBERTO resumes his feral, feverish painting. ISAKU*
> *has an internal moment.)*

ISAKU: I cannot love Alberto and Annette more. But I know that my love has upset the balance of their home. Diego has never accepted me. Diego will never accept me. Upsetting their balance has upset my balance . . . Father, mother, rest your souls. My wife, my children . . . I know I have disappointed you . . . but this is who I am. It is only through art that we can redeem ourselves.

ALBERTO: Keep looking into each other's eyes . . . Now hold hands.

ANNETTE: Alberto—

ALBERTO:— hold hands! . . . All four . . . Stop. Hold them just like that . . . Let me get closer.

ANNETTE: We can move—*(closer to you)*

ALBERTO:—I will come closer.

> *(ALBERTO violently moves his easel and materials uncomfortably closer. He resumes manically painting. Time passes.)*

ALBERTO: It still needs something.

ANNETTE: Let's change this pose.

ISAKU: Anything you need, Alberto.

ALBERTO: Anything?

ISAKU: Anything.

ALBERTO: I want you two to get naked.

ANNETTE: Naked?

ALBERTO: Annette, you have posed this way many times before.

ANNETTE: But today is . . . well, very different . . . Can we talk a moment?

ALBERTO: Of course.

> (ISAKU starts getting undressed. ALBERTO, for the first time in the play, removes his jacket and loosens his tie.)

ANNETTE: Alone.

ALBERTO: But Isaku—(is here)

ISAKU:—I'll go to Café Didot for some wine.

ALBERTO: You don't have to—(do that).

ANNETTE: —Thank you, Isaku.

> (ISAKU puts back on whatever clothing he had removed and exits.)

ANNETTE: What's wrong, Alberto?

ALBERTO: When I look at you, I see Isaku. When I think of you, I see Isaku. . . I must purge this apparition.

ANNETTE: You need to rest.

ALBERTO: Annette, all I really have to give to you, to this world, is in this room. In this room I have created a life for you and me, and for Diego. I fear I have taken this force for granted—destroying far more than I can ever create. This force of life is now a force of death. It has claimed my eyes and my memory . . . Let us get back to work before it claims my hands—

ANNETE Put yourself in the portrait, next to me, next to Isaku. . . Naked.

ALBERTO: I can't do that.

ANNETTE: We'll stand side-by-side forever.

ALBERTO: My soul is beside you, inside you, contained deep within every portrait I have ever made of you.

ANNETTE: But what about your face, your body? Alberto, you need to show this too.

ALBERTO: Nobody wants to see a lame, sterile old man—I don't even want to see my own body.

ANNETTE: I'm sorry, Alberto. I can't work on this anymore.

ALBERTO: Now you're trying to destroy me.

ANNETTE: Destroy that portrait before it destroys all of us. I have to go home. You need to get some rest. I'll bring you a new basket tomorrow, please call me if you need anything else.

> *(ANNETTE gathers her coat and the empty food basket.)*

ALBERTO: Annette . . . Please forgive me. This is the only way I know how to touch you.

ANNETTE: Say goodnight to Isaku for me.

> *(ANNETTE kisses ALBERTO and exits. ISAKU enters. He calls down the street . . .)*

ISAKU: Annette!?

ALBERTO: Isaku, let's get back to work.

ISAKU: Is she coming back?

ALBERTO: Eyes to me. Only to me.

> *End of scene.*

ACT II / Scene 3

Later that night, ANNETTE's apartment. She is in bed reading. There's a knock on the door.

ISAKU: *(off-stage)* Annette? Annette?

ANNETTE: Isaku? What time is it . . . ?

ISAKU: *(off-stage)* Please open the door.

> *(ANNETTE gets up and turns on a light to reveal that her apartment has a small, artist studio area with an empty chair, easel and sketches on the wall. ISAKU enters.)*

ISAKU: I wish you would answer your telephone—

ANNETTE:—Did you plan that session with Alberto?

ISAKU: Nobody tells Alberto what to do.

ANNETTE: He listens to some more than others.

ISAKU: I know this afternoon did not go well. But for what it's worth, Alberto and I have been working in the studio for almost twelve hours straight. Please. Come see the beginning of this powerful new sculpture.

ANNETTE: An edict from Alberto?

ISAKU: Annette, this has nothing to do with Alberto. I would like you to take a walk with me to the studio to see something that we have been working on for the past twelve hours.

ANNETTE: I cannot and will not go back there tonight.

ISAKU: Alberto is on the verge of making history. I know he's your husband, but don't lose sight of the fact that you and I, and Diego, are the only ones who have consistently captured the imagination of one of the great artists of the world. We must seize this moment.

ANNETTE: We haven't captured Alberto for a second. He has captured us.

ISAKU: In your letters, you didn't tell me you had a new home.

ANNETTE: I didn't think you were coming back so soon. There was barely enough room for Alberto . . . and Diego at the studio. There was certainly not any more room there for me.

ISAKU: He's calling this new sculpture, "Legacy."

ANNETTE: Alberto is right, only through art can there be legacy.

ISAKU: A sculpture can be a legacy, but there is no stronger legacy than a child. Annette, it's not too late.

ANNETTE: Biologically, no. Emotionally: I think our time has passed.

ISAKU: This is not about time. This is about being. Together. After father died, I thought of all the things I would like to achieve before it's my time to leave this earth. I want this legacy with you.

ANNETTE: So, you do think of me when you're back in Japan.

ISAKU: I think of you constantly.

ANNETTE: Do you ever discuss me with your wife and daughters?

ISAKU: Annette—

ANNETTE:—Do you discuss Alberto with them?

ISAKU: Annette, we have an understanding.

ANNETTE: I have an understanding with you. I have an understanding with Alberto. But neither of you have an understanding with me. Isaku I have lived my entire adult life in the shadow of Alberto. . . I can't live in that shadow any longer.

ISAKU: I do not see us as being obscured by Alberto's shadow. I see us reflected in his light. Having a child will cast a new light . . . although the old shadows will still be there.

ANNETTE: Isaku, I know you have always loved and always will love Alberto more than you love me. And I cannot share you with him anymore.

> (ISAKU is speechless . . . He finally takes in his surroundings.)

ISAKU: I see you have created your own studio here. Now you get to "dance" as much as Alberto does.

ANNETTE: I don't think anyone can keep up with Alberto. But I do what I can. Better yet, I do what I want.

ISAKU: The work is quite wonderful, Annette. Has Alberto seen these?

ANNETTE: He refuses to come here.

ISAKU: You have made a wonderful home for yourself.

ANNETTE: Thank you, Isaku.

ISAKU: Does a part of you miss living in the studio?

ANNETTE: I still stop by there every day. I straighten up; make sure he and Diego have some wine, some food. In winter I keep the furnace stoked and burning. Living here is not that different. Except now I can finally go to sleep with the light off.

ISAKU: Do you still use the calligraphy set I gave you?

ANNETTE: Not very often.

ISAKU: Who is this in the drawing?

ANNETTE: That's me. I work from mirrors and memory.

ISAKU: Who is that with you?

ANNETTE: That's you.

ISAKU: Oh. And is this one also of us?

ANNETTE: This is me. But that is someone else.

ISAKU: Annette. Can we still be together?

ANNETTE: I don't know, Isaku. I don't know.

End of scene.

ACT II / Scene 4

The Studio, the next day. ALBERTO and DIEGO are working.
A covered sculpture occupies a prominent spot.

ALBERTO: By tomorrow I think the new sculpture will be ready for a patina.

DIEGO: Have you had any more time to work on those studies for New York?

ALBERTO: The plaza isn't even built yet.

DIEGO: Father would have never squandered the golden opportunity that has fallen into your lap.

ALBERTO: Fallen into my lap? Diego. . . sometimes you shock me and disappoint me.

DIEGO: Don't speak to me of disappointment. I have always been here for you and I will always be here for you. But we're not getting any younger. I need to start devoting time to my own work.

ALBERTO: Without you, my work would have never flourished the way it has. But without me, you probably wouldn't be alive now. When you arrived in Paris you were living out a death wish of smuggling and petty crime.

DIEGO: Alberto—that was over thirty years ago!

ALBERTO: I think about my work every second I am alive——whether I am here in the studio, at the café, at the brothel, with mother in Stampa. Everything we are, everything we will ever be, starts and ends in this room. If I am cautious about New York, it is for good reason.

(ISAKU enters.)

ISAKU: Good evening, gentlemen. *(Dead silence.)* Shall I wait in Café Didot?

DIEGO: No. I will leave you two to work.

ALBERTO: Diego please stay. We're not going to work tonight. I have a new sculpture that I would like you to see. I telephoned Annette, but she's not answering.

DIEGO: Let's see your new piece.

(ALBERTO unveils the sculpture.)

ALBERTO: By combining a bust of Isaku and the body of Annette, I feel I have finally completed a sculpture to the best of my abilities.

ISAKU: Alberto . . . I don't know what to say except: Genius. Let's celebrate in Saint Germain.

ALBERTO: When Diego applies his magical patina, the sculpture will be outstanding.

THREE TREES Page 96

DIEGO: Alberto . . . I cannot and will not assist you with this sculpture.

ALBERTO: Diego!

ISAKU: Please . . . celebrate the completion of a new work.

DIEGO: Alberto, what we will celebrate at midnight is your birthday. Happy birthday, Alberto. I will see you in the morning.

(DIEGO exits . . . Pause.)

ALBERTO: We've been through much worse. We'll be fine.

ISAKU: So . . . I guess you don't need me to help you commit hara-kiri?

ALBERTO: Alchemy has been achieved. You, Isaku, are the Philosopher's stone. Hara-kiri won't be necessary. Not this time.

ISAKU: Then let us celebrate this new work and your birthday.

ALBERTO: Since my sister Otillia died in childbirth on this very day, my birthday has ceased being a day of celebration. It has become one more reminder of how tightly death and life are intertwined . . .

ISAKU:. . . Death, like life, should also be . . . if not celebrated . . . honored.

ALBERTO: I remember Otillia dying like it was yesterday.

ISAKU: Alberto. . . I've been told never to mention Picasso . . .

ALBERTO:. . . Well, you have.

ISAKU: Picasso could not have created what you have created here tonight.

ALBERTO: I have always said that if Picasso were to be tried by a jury of Art Gods, he would be sentenced to death for fraud.

ISAKU: And what, Alberto, would be your verdict?

ALBERTO: A lifetime sentence. Isaku, when this sculpture is completed, I would like for you to have it.

ISAKU: I would be most honored.

ALBERTO: This "Legacy" sculpture is for you.

ISAKU: For you and me. It is my greatest honor . . . Maestro Alberto, if Annette doesn't come tonight, may I treat you to the brothels?

ALBERTO: You would pay for me?

ISAKU: For your birthday: absolutely.

ALBERTO: Just look at us, a new work has been completed and neither of us has been conquered or destroyed. We're just . . .

ISAKU: In this moment.

ALBERTO: Yes, in this moment . . . alive together.

ISAKU: Renewal. Reinvention. This can only happen in this magical studio.

ALBERTO: The possibilities are once again endless, but this night will soon be over. You go on to Boulevard Montparnasse. I will see you later. I just need to take a walk—alone. I am sorry.

ISAKU: There is no need to apologize. Would you mind if I stayed behind?

ALBERTO: Of course. Just turn out the lights when you leave. I'll be seeing you.

ISAKU: Good night for now.

> *(ALBERTO exits. ISAKU pours another glass of wine, lights the candles in the candelabra and dims the studio lights. He becomes entranced with the sculpture.)*

ISAKU: You are greater than life itself. Deeper than love, more permanent than death, you are my soul incarnate. I poured everything I had into you and would gladly do it all over again. If I could, that would be my only activity: Giving freely of my soul to the Maestro, Alberto. Each contour and line is like the most sensuous melody and haunting harmony that man has ever heard. You are not just my soul incarnate. You are the incarnate of all of the beauty, all the "ongaku" that the world has ever known.

(DIEGO emerges. He watches ISAKU a few beats, then turns the studio lights up to full.)

DIEGO: Professor, I thought you'd be on Boulevard Montparnasse by now.

ISAKU: Did you come back to do some work?

DIEGO: I saw an unusual figure and shadow through the window.

ISAKU: Aren't all figures and shadows unusual?

DIEGO: Some comfort us, some confront us . . . Professor, how is your wife?

ISAKU: My life beyond this studio is not your concern.

DIEGO: But your actions beyond the studio are strongly influencing everything that goes on in here.

ISAKU: If you must know, Alberto has given Annette and I his blessing.

DIEGO: Alberto cannot give you his blessing. You must make your own blessing.

ISAKU: You have sat for Alberto. Do you take as much pride in the outcome as I do?

DIEGO: Alberto could be looking at a door, a wall, a mouse or a piece of cheese. It is what he sees and renders. It has nothing to do with us.

ISAKU: Why do you always debase me?

DIEGO: You have forever changed this studio without knowledge or respect for what came before.

ISAKU: If not me, it would have been someone else. Diego, I know how the world works. That's why I despise it and make my own, as in this sculpture.

DIEGO: This work of art may have come from you, but it's ours now. It's everyone's forever!

ISAKU: The first level of attraction, the first wave of intellectual engagement is all Alberto's. And yours. But if you choose to linger or meditate, convene with it; then it becomes my soul that illuminates this sculpture . . . You become flooded by the sea of my soul. The waves of my compromised love, my fractured spirit, my overprotective intellect—all of these things that crash upon the shores of my soul are the very things that make you want to look at this sculpture; To touch it, be one with it. In this moment you are beyond Alberto's studio, beyond this mortal world. You are in the immortal world of my soul. No convention, curator or institution. This sculpture is a tribute to a force that is much greater than art or war.

DIEGO: And just what is this force, Professor?

ISAKU: My love.

DIEGO: Annette has never loved you and never will.

ISAKU: Diego, this sculpture is not about the love that Annette and I share. It is a testament to the love I share with Alberto.

>   *(DIEGO grabs the sculpture and treats it like a weapon or a hostage.)*

DIEGO: With a few flecks of his blade, he could have turned your head into Annette's or mine.

ISAKU: Put the sculpture down.

DIEGO: Knowing Alberto, he will probably destroy this in the morning anyway.

ISAKU: That is Alberto's right.

DIEGO: Do you think Alberto is the only one who can play God, creating and destroying at will?

ISAKU: This has nothing to do with God. This has only to do with us. What will we leave behind? What will you give this world? Please: Put the sculpture down.

DIEGO: The world will take what it wants from me and spit the rest right back in my face.

ISAKU: Diego, we have brought some beauty into this world. That is more than most can say. Put the sculpture down.

DIEGO: This process has been going on for centuries before us. It will go on for centuries after us.

ISAKU: In that way, you and I are both superfluous. I know you never wanted me to be in Alberto's heart. That was not my intention. But it has happened. You've said, "we make our own blessing." You can destroy your brother's sculpture, but you will never change his heart.

DIEGO: Every piece in this studio begins with Alberto. But nothing, not one thing, gets finished without passing through my hands. Professor, this sculpture will never, ever, get finished. What Alberto and I must finish up, are the sculptures for New York. This is a once in a lifetime opportunity. We cannot afford any further distractions. Professor, I am going to put this sculpture down and go home. When I return in the morning, I respectfully ask that you not be here. Is that understood?

ISAKU: Yes, it is understood.

(DIEGO gracefully places the sculpture on the studio floor.)

ISAKU: Before I leave . . . May I take some of the dust from the floor?

DIEGO: Do you mean that?

ISAKU: With all of my heart and soul.

DIEGO: Be my guest.

(DIEGO exits. ISAKU gets down on all fours and starts savoring handfuls of dust from the studio floor. End of scene.)

ACT II / Scene 5

The next morning, ALBERTO and DIEGO are putting the candelabra and other interiors back into storage and setting up for a painting session. The "Isaku/Annette" sculpture is prominently displayed next to an empty chair.

ALBERTO: This is unlike Isaku to be late.

DIEGO: Maybe he's still celebrating.

ALBERTO: Do you think?

DIEGO: Alberto, I was only joking.

ALBERTO: Without him, my work would have died. I would have died.

DIEGO: But look at what he has done to us.

(ANNETTE enters.)

ANNETTE: Isaku has gone back to Japan.

ALBERTO: Impossible! I just paid for an additional month at the hotel.

ANNETTE: Here is your refund and here's a note from Isaku. It's addressed to you only.

ALBERTO: Let me see this.

(As ALBERTO opens the letter, ISAKU appears on stage and reads his own letter aloud.)

ISAKU: To My Dearest Maestro Alberto: In Japan, we sculpt the branches of a tree to grow in three ways: One for the souls in the sky above; A second on an even keel for man on earth; and the third for those in the netherworld below. With the Maestro, his beautiful wife and his invaluable brother, you have the three branches you need to support and sustain your tree. I do not want to upset that balance of trinity anymore. I have been blessed to meet all of you and I will never forget a single day spent with the three of you. I remain your humble seedling. Love, Isaku.

(ISAKU disappears. ALBERTO crumples the letter and throws it to the ground.)

ALBERTO: So, it comes to this. After giving everything I had, everything. He can't even come to the studio and tell me to my face that he is leaving.

DIEGO: Alberto, we must move on.

ALBERTO: He didn't even wait for his sculpture to be completed . . . What did I do to make him leave?

ANNETTE: You did nothing.

DIEGO: We make our own blessing, Alberto.

(ALBERTO picks up and smoothens out the crumpled letter.)

ALBERTO: My work has never been so alive. How do we replace this . . . Isaku?

ANNETTE: All we can do is create new work.

DIEGO: Perhaps we can revisit the studies for the New York sculptures.

ALBERTO: I would sooner stop making art than work further on those studies.

DIEGO: Fine. I just wish you had made this decision long ago. It would have saved so much time.

ALBERTO: More time to devote to your furniture?

DIEGO: Time to make furniture. Time to commit petty crimes. Time to smuggle illegal goods. My time, Alberto, to pursue whatever I please

ALBERTO: Then go to it. And when you make your furniture. Please sign them Diego, and Diego only.

DIEGO: I shouldn't sign them, Diego Giacometti?

ALBERTO: Only Diego. We cannot afford to have Pierre's New York clientele confuse our identities.

DIEGO: When Pierre's New York clientele come to Paris, it will be very easy to tell us apart . . . Starting today, we will be working in separate studios. Goodbye, Annette.

(DIEGO exits.)

ALBERTO: Diego!

ANNETTE: Alberto, come here.

(ANNETTE comforts ALBERTO.)

ALBERTO: I have never seen Diego like this . . . Now Isaku's gone too . . .

ANNETTE: Just like some sculptures, some relationships were only meant to exist for a brief time. Look to the new. There's still history to be made in New York. Please, Alberto, give those studies one more look.

ALBERTO: For you, I will. This is for you and this is for Diego. I am through here.

End of scene.

EPILOGUE

Tokyo, 1966. ISAKU sits in his meditation room before a bust that bears his likeness. He is once again draped in a mourning kimono. As he chooses a letter to read, the others appear before him like spirits.

ISAKU: Upon the Maestro's passing, I received a letter from Annette.

ANNETTE: Dear Isaku, I always thought I would see you one more time. Then we could sort things out face to face. That never happened. Alberto and I had a wonderful life together. But I would not call our marriage a thing of beauty. I have often given you too much credit and too much blame for the final years. When Alberto died, I had a very strong feeling. I wrapped all of your beautiful letters in brown paper— just like the paper that the butcher wraps your meat in. I marched straight down Boulevard Saint Michael to the Seine to dump them into the river. But then I remembered us walking and talking in the cafes, on the bridges. I decided to keep them. All of them. The feelings they evoke are not all good. But they are all strong. They keep me alive. And in a strange way, they keep Alberto alive. Love always, Annette.

ISAKU: My final communiqué from Paris came from Diego. It was a month after the Maestro's passing.

DIEGO: Dear Professor: Upon returning from Alberto's funeral I went straight to the studio and removed the

towels that Alberto had wrapped around his last
sculpture. Miraculously, the towels stayed just moist
enough to keep the sculpture from cracking—even in the
bitter January cold. This work was a full body sculpture
of a friend who has trouble walking, so he is posed on his
knees. Annette and I will place Alberto's final sculpture
on his final resting place. We will do that in April, when
the valley of Stampa is back in sunlight and no longer
engulfed in shadows. If you would care to join us, I think
that would make Alberto happy. While we did not see
eye to eye, I respect what you did for my brother's art.
That is what he was here for. That is what I am here for.
Am I my brother's keeper? No. I am not his keeper, nor
is he my keeper. We are brothers. Nothing more,
certainly nothing less. Respectfully, Diego.

(DIEGO and ANNETTE drop to their knees—
emulating ALBERTO's final sculpture.)

ISAKU: In European painting, the person is the primary
focus. The person will usually be the largest object in the
tableaux. But in Asian painting, the landscape dominates
the tableaux, and the people are but small,
complimentary figures to that landscape. It is as if the
artist is already seeing a bigger world beyond his own
mortal life. The last time I walked the Louvre with
Alberto, we meditated on Rembrandt's "Three Trees."

ALBERTO: Between this world and the next, you will
pass three trees. When I die, I imagine I will see a
landscape just like this one. Just who or what those three
trees are changes every day. Every night. Every time my

hands touch the clay, or my brush touches the canvas, I will try to make those three trees my own. Every time I look at "Three Trees" I am reminded that there is more than enough for me to do before I die . . .

> *(ISAKU rises and gently showers ALBERTO, ANNETTE and DIEGO with handfuls of dust from Alberto's studio as he chants/incants.)*

ISAKU: Maestro Alberto, it is from your dust that our essence was created and immortalized. We will always be here for you. Maestro Alberto, we will always be here for you. Maestro Alberto, we will always be here for you.

> *(ISAKU kneels down alongside ANNETTE and DIEGO. ALBERTO comes downstage and addresses the audience directly.)*

ALBERTO: Here we are . . . Eyes to me . . . Beautiful. Hold that.

END OF PLAY.

CPSIA information can be obtained
at www.ICGtesting.com
Printed in the USA
LVHW101601181221
706576LV00018B/1378